Praise for Accomplished

If you've spent even one minute thinking - *knowing* - that there is something more out there just waiting for you to grab ahold of it but you're not sure *how*, then this book is for you. The journey to achieving whatever true success is for you starts with mindset, then getting to know one's self, and finally, being able to execute. Through a series of lessons and exercises, Jodi has every step laid out for her reader, all placed brilliantly with confidence, integrity and a sense of humor.

Kate Erickson
Entrepreneur on Fire
www.eofire.com

With 15 years of sales experience, I spent every day sharing my winning sales strategies with entrepreneurs around the world. But, after years of working with entrepreneurs, I now realize how important it is to develop a winning mindset. If the person does not have the mindset to believe in herself, she will not implement those winning strategies.

With her psychology background, Jodi created this great book filled with practical advice to guide all women from dreaming to doing. I would strongly recommend any women who wants to take the lead in this world to read this book.

i

Melinda Chen
Women Making Big Sales
www.womenmakingbigsales.com

With *Accomplished*, Jodi Flynn provides a clear plan for any woman who is serious about making her life a masterpiece. As a coach to professional women – and as someone who has worked on her own limiting beliefs and mindset - Jodi understands at a deep level what's required to make the breakthroughs that expand your life's possibilities and the results you achieve.

Using a conversational, engaging style, Jodi positions herself as a guide, walking beside the reader, not as a remote guru dispensing advice. She has faced her own challenges, struggles and setbacks, and her willingness to be honest about them makes her immensely relatable to the reader. She understands first-hand how lack of self-care, reactions to stress, and attempts to hide the "real you" can prevent you from showing up powerfully, no matter what position you hold. The clear steps she outlines, combined with the exercises and resources she provides throughout, make this a compelling handbook for creating the kind of life you really want. If you implement Jodi's ideas, you'll be more likely to identify and achieve your life's purpose. Indeed, you will be ACCOMPLISHED.

Meredith Bell, President
Performance Support Systems, Inc.

ii

Jodi expertly guides you through the process of understanding who you are, discovering what you're capable of, and conquering your fears ... with personality and heart. She delivers reality checks in such an artful way that you wonder how on Earth you had your blinders on for so long! By the end of the book, I had a new mindset on balance and was able to intentionally set goals for the next phase of my business.

Nicole Boucher
nboucher.com

ACCOMPLISHED

HOW TO GO FROM DREAMING TO DOING

Hello, I'm Jodi Flynn

Though a Psychology major in college, I spent the early part of my career as an executive in mutual fund operations. During my work in that industry, I found I flourished in the areas of supervising, mentoring, project management and team building.

It was also during this time I discovered my personal mission – to listen for, bring out and nurture other people's *Superpowers* so they could use them to their advantage. I knew I was meant to focus on helping others discover success and fulfillment in their careers and businesses.

In 2010, I seized the opportunity to train as a Professional Coach through the Institute of Professional Excellence in Coaching (iPEC).

Today, as the Founder of Women Taking the Lead I host the top-ranked Podcast, lead a thriving community of entrepreneurial minded women, and I work with individuals and groups focusing on those often overlooked qualities that, if not developed, prevent us from achieving our goals: mindset, confidence, self-leadership, communication and relationship building.

I am a passionate and focused mentor and coach, providing my clients the structure necessary to challenge personal barriers and create the lives, careers and businesses they desire.

I take pride in 'walking my talk', taking on challenges that push me outside of my own comfort zone – from following my passion for a career that moved me away from my family and friends to a new state, running a marathon, starting a business, launching the Women Taking the Lead Podcast and...writing a book!

I feel the same fear others do when "putting myself out there" but I know that is the path to living full-out, and I love to encourage others to overcome their fears and do the same. I bring like-minded women together who understand what you're going through and are there to support you and share in your goals and visions.

ACCOMPLISHED:

How to Go From Dreaming to Doing

By Jodi Flynn

First published in 2016

ISBN 978-0692806975

www.WomenTakingTheLead.com

This book is dedicated to my parents, Richard and Catherine Flynn, whom have lived their lives according to their values. Without their love, support and challenge I could not have grown to be the woman I am today.

FREE Bonus Resources

Accomplished: How to Go from Dreaming to Doing

WomenTakingTheLead.com/resources

I'm not just releasing a book; I'm giving access to my signature coaching system that includes videos, downloadable worksheets and other bonus content so you can dive deeper and get the most out of your experience with this book.

I recommend you sign up now so all the bonus materials you need to engage with the content of this book are at your fingertips. It is all organized by chapters of this book so it will be easy to find as you read along.

I'll be adding to the free resources on the website overtime, so be sure to get registered and keep the website below handy because you've got some things you want to accomplish.

WomenTakingTheLead.com/resources

"Our deepest fear is not that we are inadequate. Our deepest fear is that we are powerful beyond measure. It is our light, not our darkness that most frightens us. We ask ourselves, 'Who am I to be brilliant, gorgeous, talented, fabulous?' Actually, who are you not to be? You are a child of God. Your playing small does not serve the world. There is nothing enlightened about shrinking so that other people won't feel insecure around you. We are all meant to shine, as children do. We were born to make manifest the glory of God that is within us. It's not just in some of us; it's in everyone. And as we let our own light shine, we unconsciously give other people permission to do the same. As we are liberated from our own fear, our presence automatically liberates others."

~Marianne Williamson,

"Security is mostly a superstition. It does not exist in nature, nor do the children of men as a whole experience it. Avoiding danger is no safer in the long run than outright exposure. Life is either a daring adventure, or nothing."

~ Helen Keller

"I am a little pencil in the hand of a writing God who is sending a love letter to the world."

~ Saint Teresa

CONTENTS

AUTHOR'S PREFACE

This book is for the woman who feels misunderstood because she's not satisfied with "good enough." She craves excellence and desires to always bring the best forward in herself, those around her and any group or organization she belongs to.

She's smart, hardworking, and adaptable to the people and situations around her. These qualities have made her successful, but that's not good enough for her. She has a vision of success that's bigger than where she is now. It goes beyond wanting it, she feels called to it — she's mission driven. Her vision of success is real, but she doesn't have it in her possession yet, and it frustrates her.

If this is you there are probably some other things that are true about you as well.

You are driven and, though those who know you would tell you how successful you are, you crave a level of achievement that has eluded you thus far. Because of this, loved ones sometimes don't understand the sacrifices you make, the insistence to constantly tweak and improve and, sometimes, your desire to go at it alone.

You've probably achieved your current success largely due to your own grit. People may have helped you along the way, but they were willing to help due to your work ethic, problem solving skills, and adaptability within a team.

I'm guessing you are less likely to fully trust and rely on others for your success. You may have a small team, but you're likely working a lot harder than anyone else. It's tough to delegate because others won't put the same dedication into a task as you will.

I'm here to say you will get there. You will achieve that level of success. It is possible and within your grasp.

My mission is to help entrepreneurial-minded women, just like you, go BIG with confidence, integrity, and a sense of humor.

It's why I'm writing this book.

My mission wasn't formed on a whim. I didn't choose the words because they sounded good together. Each word rings true to me and my values. When I removed a word, the statement was incomplete, and when I added a word, it was overdone.

Entrepreneurial:

1. a person who organizes and manages any enterprise, especially a business, usually with considerable initiative and risk.

2. an employer of productive labor; contractor.

3. to deal with or initiate as an entrepreneur.

4. to act as an entrepreneur.

Many people think of entrepreneurs as being business owners, but there's a new term that has developed in the last several years: intrapreneur.

An intrapreneur is a game-changer within an organization. They zero in on what's missing and provide solutions. They treat the company they work for like their own. They have buy-in, dedication, and a vision of the future. They're emotionally involved in the wellness of their organization.

When I talk about entrepreneurial-minded women I'm referring to both entrepreneurs and intrapreneurs.

Confidence:

1. the state of feeling certain about the truth of something.

2. a feeling of self-assurance arising from one's appreciation of one's own abilities or qualities.

There are no guarantees. Confidence isn't being cocksure of an outcome. It's trusting that, whatever comes at you, you will be able to deal with it and/or learn from it.

This is why you will often hear me saying that confidence comes *after* action. You have to test out your mettle a bit before you gain that self-assurance in your abilities.

Confidence allows you to stretch your comfort zone, which in turn creates more opportunities for you.

Integrity:

1. the quality of being honest and having strong moral principles.

2. the state of being whole and undivided.

Integrity is the foundation of who you are and what you do. It is your moral compass. It means being true: true to yourself, true to your word, true to your convictions.

Without integrity it all falls apart. When an object has integrity, it is considered "structurally sound." You can trust it will do what it is designed to do. When a person has integrity you can trust what they say and that they live according to their values.

Living with integrity decreases your overall stress level, increases your personal power, and attracts like-minded people to you.

Sense of Humor:

1. the ability to perceive humor or appreciate a joke.

"A person without a sense of humor is like a wagon without springs. It's jolted by every pebble on the road." ~ Henry Ward Beecher

"I realize that humor isn't for everyone. It's only for people who want to have fun, enjoy life, and feel alive." ~ Anne Wilson Schaef

"Humor is mankind's greatest blessing." ~ Mark Twain

"Like a welcome summer rain, humor may suddenly cleanse and cool the earth, the air and you." ~ Langston Hughes

"The world is full of a lot of fear and a lot of negativity, and a lot of judgment. I just think people need to start shifting into joy and happiness. As corny as it sounds, we need to make a shift." ~ Ellen DeGeneres

"Common sense and a sense of humor are the same thing, moving at different speeds. A sense of humor is just common sense, dancing." ~ Clive James

"I love people who make me laugh. I honestly think it's the thing I like most, to laugh. It cures a multitude of ills. It's probably the most important thing in a person." ~ Audrey Hepburn

If you are going to go big, to dare to change the world and be seen, you're going to need your sense of humor.

Be a gift to yourself and those around you. Develop your sense of the ridiculous and share it kindly.

So there you have it. This book is designed to help you go big with confidence, integrity and a sense of humor. It's my belief that when those pieces are in place, the rest will work itself out.

There's a method to my madness, so when you are reading a section or being asked to do a particular exercise and your thoughts go to, "what does this have to do with...?", do it anyway.

The mindset and actions that lead us to new understanding is often counterintuitive. It is when we are taken outside of our ordinary experience that our filter (beliefs) will reveal itself.

Know that I'm in this with you. I want to be your buddy as you go through this resource.

****If you would like added support there are opportunities in **The Accomplished Community** to connect with others and to find an accountability buddy if you'd like to team up with someone who is reading this book at the same time you are.

Type this link into your browser to get more information:
womentakingthelead.com/accomplished-community

INTRODUCTION

"The work we do is a reflection of who we are.

If we're sloppy at it, it's because we're sloppy inside. If we're late at it, it's because we're late inside. If we are bored by it, it is because we're bored inside, with ourselves, not with the work. The work can be a piece of art when done by an artist. So the job here is not outside of ourselves, but inside of ourselves.

How we do our work becomes a mirror of how we are inside.

In the process, the work you do becomes you. And you become the force that breathes life into the idea behind the work. You become the creator of the work you do."

~Michael Gerber, The E-Myth

As Michael Gerber so eloquently states, the quality of our outer world is a reflection of our inner world, yet most of us spend very little time reflecting on what's happening in our inner world. If you're like me, it's hard to sit still long enough to contemplate your inner thoughts and feelings. After all, there's so much to do, and you're not done with your day yet! You know reflection is important, so you give it some time here and there, and you have some basic understanding of how you think and feel... but the reality is that you've barely scratched the surface.

Your inner world is the foundation of your successes and failures. What you don't understand is that it's the driving force behind your results. I know this because if you truly understood your inner world, you wouldn't be reading a book on how to become accomplished.

"We see the world not as it is. We see the world as we are." ~ Anais Nin

Here's another way to think about it. We are film projectors projecting our inner world onto the world around us. We think what we are taking in is what is real, but we're really taking in what we're projecting out.

Yes, things happen that are unplanned, people don't always do what they say they would — but the meaning, the intention and the emotion around the situation? That all came from you. It colored the canvas of facts and gave it drama. And your mind tricked you into believing the drama was the facts, and you acted accordingly.

Our minds are very powerful, yet there are billions of bits of information coming at us all the time. The mind needs to make sense of it all, and it uses a simple system to filter the overload of information. Knowing this, we can learn how to use its formula to our advantage.

When we were young children, the world was very confusing, and we depended on those around us to make sense of what was happening. With each new experience came new words and explanations. Our brains started to notice patterns and began wiring itself accordingly. All new information began being processed by the brain's "what we already know" filter. Each new experience is compared to some similar previous experience, labeled, cataloged, and added to the filter.

Think of this filter as contact lenses that rest weightless over your eyes. Eventually, and very slowly, everything you came to understand and believe about the world and the people around you colored the lenses resting on your eyes. Now, each new experience is seen through a colored filter and can only be understood based on what has happened in the past.

You think you are seeing everything as it really is but the truth is you are seeing everything through a filter — your colored contact lenses that you don't even realize are there. You, the film projector, shine a pure white light through the colored lenses of your beliefs and what you see is a result of what is projected out, shaping how you respond.

And the cycle continues becoming a self-fulfilling prophecy, your inner world determining the results you can achieve in the outer world.

Every day we interact with others wearing their own colored contact lenses. And, they don't realize they're not seeing things as they really are either.

For instance, one person's life experience has lent them to believe that being on time is being early. Another person's life experience has taught them that it is disruptive to the host to arrive early and it's better to arrive a few minutes late. Both are justified in their world view but you can see where this might create conflict and make it hard for these two individuals to work together. If they don't have an understanding of the way the other person is viewing the situation there will be a tendency to judge them unfavorably.

There's no getting rid of your contact lenses. It's just how our brain works. It's not all doom and gloom, though. Now that you know you are wearing colored contact lenses, you can decide which beliefs you want to color your lenses and create a projection that empowers you, makes you happy, and allows you to take action toward your goals.

One of the goals of this book is to help you to identify the beliefs that color your contact lenses (and, therefore, the world around you), so you can keep the ones that serve you and examine and redesign the ones that hold you back and keep you from reaching your goals.

It won't always be obvious that this is what I'm doing but I'm going to ask you to trust me and follow this book to the end. "There is a method to my madness," I like to tell my clients.

Some of the other goals I have for this book are to help you:

1. Identify your knee-jerk reactions to what's coming at you (and that ends up keeping you from your goals).

2. Have a new understanding of who you really are and what you're capable of.

3. Create goals and a plan in alignment with who you really are and what you are capable of.

PART I:
BELIEVE YOU WILL
BE SUCCESSFUL

"Whether you think you can, or you think you can't –
you're right."

~ Henry Ford

Chapter 1:

Imagine the Future and Set the Intention to Succeed

"If you want something you've never had, you must be willing to do something you've never done."

~ Thomas Jefferson

A Vision for Success

Every woman I work with has a vision of herself achieving success. There is some specific image in her mind that represents the very moment when she's "made it".

Not only does she see herself achieving success, she imagines what it will feel like when it happens.

Because the image is so real for her, she lives like it's a foregone conclusion. She might be facing obstacles now, but she knows that success is hers to be had. It's just a matter of time and hard work.

Her vision and the success story in her mind is why she is able to keep going, even if her current reality doesn't support her vision.

In his best-selling business book *The eMyth*, Michael Gerber calls this process "The Dreaming Room." He explains at length how important it is for business owners to spend time away from their business to dream and imagine the possibilities. This is the time when ideas are formed and solutions are created.

Take, for example, these three stories from an article in *Entrepreneur* magazine:

1. Boxing legend Muhammad Ali stressed the importance of seeing himself victorious long before the actual fight.

2. As a struggling young actor, Jim Carrey wo[.] himself being the greatest actor in the world.

3. Michael Jordan always took the last shot in his ... before he ever took one in real life.

The question is posed: If you can't picture yourself achieving success in your mind how will you do it in real life?

Sometimes I struggle with visualizing success, but I've found a helpful system for guiding me through the process of imagining myself having already achieved success, and I'm sharing it with you.

Find a quiet spot where you can sit in solitude, away from any distractions for 15 minutes to listen to this audio guide.

Type this link into your browser to access the bonus materials: **womentakingthelead.com/resources**

Welcome back, and I hope that helped you to see and feel the kind of success you want in your life. If you struggled with this exercise, that's okay.

Sometimes if there is too much noise in our head, it's hard to really get into an exercise like this. Shake it off and try again another time when you don't feel the world pulling at you. So, go for a walk, go about your day, and come back and do it again.

If you don't have an image and a feeling of what success will look like you'll continue to trudge along hoping that,

11

.e day, things will get better. I don't want that for you. I want you to be mission driven. When you have a mission, you have confidence, energy, and a clear path in front of you.

Intend the Outcome

Setting an intention is setting your mind to an outcome and then imaging how you will *feel* when you've achieved it.

When you set an intention, you put your energy behind a goal and stay flexible as to how it is achieved. You allow things to unfold without trying to control them.

This energy will allow you to respond rather than react if things don't go according to plan. It's a higher state of consciousness that allows space for the unexpected, unplanned, pleasant, and unpleasant surprises.

Intention is not tenacity but it allows for tenacity. Intention is more like calm conviction.

When you intend for something to happen, there is no giving up. There is no evidence convincing enough to make you believe that the outcome you have imagined will not come about.

Chapter 2:

Commit to it Like Your Life Depends Upon it

"Until one is committed, there is hesitancy, the chance to draw back, always ineffectiveness. Concerning all acts of initiative and creation, there is one elementary truth the ignorance of which kills countless ideas and splendid plans: that **the moment one definitely commits oneself, then providence moves too**. All sorts of things occur to help one that would never otherwise have occurred. A whole stream of events issues from the decision, raising in one's favor all manner of unforeseen incidents, meetings and material assistance which no man could have dreamed would have come his way. Whatever you can do or dream you can, begin it. Boldness has genius, power and magic in it. Begin it now. "

~ Johann Wolfgang von Goethe

Many of us have, in our heads, ideas of events, achievements, or recognitions that we'd like to occur, receive, or have.

Let's call these wishes.

We have the thought but no action or very little action to back it up. We wish and wish and wish... and soon we notice all of the time passing by without our wishes granted.

Every now and again, we may take tentative steps toward our dream. We try something new; we buy a lottery ticket or start a conversation with an attractive stranger. But when it doesn't work, we go back to wishing.

If you want to achieve your heart's desire, it will require changes — changes that you must commit to.

We all know change is difficult, but here's a secret: change is only difficult when you haven't committed to it. Making changes you don't *really* want to make is exhausting, stressful, and defeating. The reality is that your lack of commitment is the only thing making change hard.

When you are committed, you don't question it, you don't resist it. You throw yourself into it full force. You may acknowledge the difficulties, but they don't stop you. Instead, you can see past them. You're much more aware of the benefits, simply because you're looking for them.

For the first 30 years of my life, I wanted to be physically fit. I envied the girls who could eat what they wanted and still looked great in a bikini every summer. I was not designed that way and knew that I had to take a different path.

I resented it. I resisted it.

Physical fitness was going to require a lot more than I was willing to give. So I'd go through stages of working out semi-regularly and watching what I ate and then go on strike. I would eat what I wanted and would not work out (not even for a minute).

The consequences to my body were self-evident and damaging. In my 20s, my weight fluctuated between 165 and over 200 pounds.

Around the age of 30, I began semi-private fitness training with a group of friends. I was about 40 pounds overweight — having bounced back from 60 pounds over — and had recently started to run on the treadmill for a couple of minutes at a time.

I was committed to this group, but more importantly, I was committed to myself. I told myself that, at 30, it was now or never. I would never have a better opportunity to do it again. I signed up for local 5k races, then a 10k, and in October of the next year I completed a half-marathon.

Within a month of completing the half-marathon, I decided I was going to run the full marathon the next year. There was no question in my mind — that race was going to happen.

As the holidays arrived I made some BIG changes. I cut out sugar, white flour, processed foods, fast food, and, yup, alcohol. At this point, I was still 15 pounds above the ideal starting weight for my official training in April.

Was it hard?

It was a challenge at times, but it was a lot easier than I expected it to be.

I didn't eat those foods anymore. Period. It wasn't up for discussion, so I didn't waffle over any decisions that needed to be made. When offered something I couldn't eat, I'd politely say, "no, thank you". If a dish I wanted on the menu had an ingredient that I couldn't eat, I would order the dish without it.

I trained through the summer, including vacations, holidays, birthday parties, random barbeques and all the good things that go with summer.

Did I cheat?

Nope.

Nothing was bigger or more important than being at my absolute optimal for every workout or run along the journey.

Was I resentful?

Nope.

As the pounds dropped away and my body got tighter and stronger, I had my progress to comfort me.

Every other week I did a longer distance run and felt the victory each and every time. And every time I put on my new smaller-sized clothes, it felt like a pat on the back and a high-five. What was cake to that feeling?

I had a network of people who became inspired by my goal. They appreciated and admired my steadfast resolve. They supported my diet and my lifestyle and offered to do training runs with me so I would have companionship along the way.

If I had only been half as committed, my support system would not have been the same. I would not have inspired anyone to do anything outside of their normal routine. It was my commitment that inspired them. The actions I took were in alignment with my commitment; they could see it and wanted to be part of it.

At the age of 30, I became a runner, and, at the age of 31, I became a marathon runner. Without my commitment to it and to myself, it never would have happened.

Commitment is a game-changer.

It's not sexy and a lot of people don't like to talk about it, but that's the reason why many of us are living a shadow of the life we want to be living. It's because we haven't fully committed to it.

"The decision to succeed comes before a plan." ~ Jay Baer

The moment you commit to a goal and take action in alignment with that goal, following through without knowing the outcome, is the moment that doors will start to open.

Until you commit and take decisive action, you're on the sidelines and nobody knows what you need. They don't know how to contribute to you.

There is boldness and surety that comes with commitment. And it is that boldness and surety that inspires others to support, if not join you, on your path.

Examples of commitments:

1. I am committed to reading at least one non-fiction book a month to focus on my professional development.

2. I am committed to meditating each morning for at least 5-10 minutes.

3. I am committed to increasing my revenue by $2000/month by December.

4. I am committed to hiring an assistant/house cleaner/landscaper so I can focus more time on what's important to me.

5. I am committed to shutting off my computer by 5 pm each night.

If you still find yourself hesitating over making that commitment, you're not alone.

This commitment is to you and to you alone.

As women it's so easy for us to advocate and commit to others but when it comes to doing this for ourselves – we back away.

Why is that?

I believe it's because we are hard-wired to take care of others. We are also nurtured to do this. We are rewarded as children for doing thoughtful things for others but not for speaking up and asking for what we need or want.

We may even have had an experience where we were chastised for asking for what we needed or wanted.

When I was growing up, making sacrifices for others was always acknowledged and celebrated. And it should be – it's wonderful.

But there is something else that I believe must come first. There has to be a commitment to you and, as much as I cringe saying this because of my conditioning, you have to come first.

If you don't come first, everything else will suffer as a consequence.

I struggle with this one. To be completely transparent, there is a part of me that resists commitment altogether.

I sometimes joke that it's because I'm a Sagittarius. I love my freedom too much to tie myself down to too many commitments and that's probably the reason why I'm single.

I make plans to meet up with friends for dinner, and I'm really excited about it. Then the day comes and, by the afternoon, I am overwhelmed with the desire to get into my pajamas and watch reruns of The West Wing for the evening.

I feel a pang of regret that I've made plans for dinner but my commitment and my integrity – that I've given my word – eventually wins over and, instead of pajamas and TV, I go out with friends and enjoy a good meal, and I don't regret it.

Don't get me wrong; it's not always something fun that I've committed to. Sometimes it's just the satisfaction that I was true to my word that rewards me for overcoming my desire to binge watch Netflix.

Making and keeping commitments, especially to yourself, will help you to keep moving forward and in the direction of your dreams, despite any short-lived cravings to play it small, play it safe and play it comfortable.

Here are some things you can do if you struggle with making and keeping commitments to yourself:

1. Make sure what you are committing to is 100% relevant.

How often have you found yourself committed to something that has no real value or meaning to you? These are the times you find yourself saying, "I don't even know why I agreed to this?"

Be very clear on what you value and what your goals are. Only make commitments that are a reflection of them.

Everything else is a "no." And if you find yourself saying "yes" when you really wanted to say "no", take a look in the mirror and uncover what it was that compelled you to say yes. This can often range from a need to be liked to avoiding conflict.

Just know that whatever reason compelled you, in that moment, to say "yes" — you gave it more power than your values and your goals. Think about how you can handle that situation differently in the future so when it comes up again, and it will, you will be able to navigate it with more power and ease.

If your commitment is relevant, if it reflects your values and goals, it will be much easier to overcome the urges to break your commitment. You can remind yourself why this commitment is important and how it will improve your life in the long-term.

2. Focus on what you'll enjoy about the commitment.

I'm in a phase right now where I have gotten off-track with my workouts, and I'm trying to get back to the level of fitness I was at over the summer. Over the holidays, and when I was in an intense period of catching up after the holidays, my workouts took a nosedive and I knew I needed to get back into a rhythm.

Knowing this would be a struggle, I committed to — at the very least — getting 10-15 minutes of cardio in everyday to start building up my endurance again. Easy, right?

Wrong.

Every day there was "one more thing and one more thing" that needed to get done before I could do my workout and, before I knew it, there wasn't even 10 minutes left for a workout. In fact, I was running late and barely had time to take a shower and get ready before I need to race out the door.

When I took a look at the list of things that made up the "one more thing" they were all tasks that could have waited. I was just using them to procrastinate because I hated being reminded by my workout that I was no longer as physically fit as I once was. I didn't look forward to it, and so I was avoiding it to my own detriment.

I made a conscious effort to change my mindset and focus on what I do enjoy about my workout: it's 10-15 minutes just for me, I get to listen to my favorite music or podcasts, I can focus on the progress I'm making, I can enjoy the endorphin rush and the feeling of satisfaction that comes when I'm done, and I can check my workout off my list. And it's not hanging over my head for the rest of the day that I skipped my simple workout yet again.

3. Ask others to hold you accountab your commitment.

Many people resist accountability because it sounds like being taken to task and is just another way to feel bad about making and breaking a commitment.

However, accountability is only meant to be a check-in and not a disciplinary hearing. It's an opportunity to communicate the status of your commitment and make any adjustments or recommit if necessary.

Accountability is for you, not for the other person.

Gretchen Rubin, the author of *The Happiness Project* and *Better Than Before* and co-host of the podcast *Happier*, talks often about the four tendencies when it comes to forming and keeping habits: upholder, questioner, obliger and rebel.

You can go to Gretchen's site to take the quiz: **https://gretchenrubin.com/happiness_pro ject/2015/01/ta-da-the-launch-of-my-quiz-on-the-four-tendencies-learn-about-yourself/**

You can also use this short link: **http://buff.ly/2edbrUT**

I'm an obliger, and I'm not surprised. That means that I am motivated to make others happy. I don't like to disappoint people so accountability works great for me.

However, if your tendency is to rebel then accountability will probably not work for you.

As an obliger I also have to be cautious of over-committing, which I do often, because overcommitting will cause stress, resentment and, ultimately, backing out of commitments.

Questioners will want to know everything about the commitment before they agree to it and Upholders will resist new commitments unless they can give 100% to it because they will give 100% and then some once they've committed.

Know what works for you and set yourself up for success.

And lastly...

4. Choose yourself every day.

I had a conversation with my father one day about marriage and the long haul and getting through tough times. In his wisdom, my father shared that a commitment was not something you set and forget. It takes thoughtfulness, care, and nurturing.

He told me that he chooses my mother every day when he wakes up. He recommits himself to her every day.

That's the kind of love we need to have for ourselves as well. We need to choose ourselves every day.

Every day, regardless of how you feel, you need to commit to honoring your relationship with yourself.

This is how you develop self-worth and personal power.

You are worth the commitment.

"Frank O'Connor, the Irish writer, tells in one of his books how, as a boy, he and his friends would make their way across the countryside, and when they came to an orchard wall that seemed too high and too doubtful to try and too difficult to permit their voyage to continue, they took off their hats and tossed them over the wall — and then they had no choice but to follow them." ~ John F. Kennedy

Here's how you toss your hat over the wall: Tell everyone you know what you're committing to and when you plan to have accomplished it.

What is one commitment you have or will make to yourself going forward? Write down your GO BIG goal.

Type this link into your browser to access the bonus materials: **womentakingthelead.com/resources** or write it down in on a blank piece of paper.

Make sure to write it big so it catches your eye often and hang it up where you can see it.

Chapter 3:

Self-care, Worthiness and Confidence

"This above all: to thine own self be true,

And it must follow, as the night the day,

Thou canst not then be false to any man."

~ William Shakespeare, Hamlet

Now that you have committed to honoring yourself and making your needs a priority, you need to model that for others. You may be clear of your worthiness, but they are not.

When we deprive ourselves of special attention, recognition, and rewards, we send a message to ourselves and others about our value. If you are not considerate of yourself, no one else will be.

In episode 25 of *Women Taking the Lead,* Christy Monson stated as her mantra, "You teach people how to treat you," and I have been passing that wisdom on ever since.

How do you send the message that you are worthy and others need to respect you? By taking excellent care of yourself.

A woman who takes excellent care of herself garners respect.

A clear sign that another person wants to have power over you is that they will in some way put you in a position where you will sacrifice your own needs for them without any reciprocation.

What comes to mind is the boss who is constantly asking you to work late. The request is, in and of itself, fine. However, what is their reciprocation? What do they follow up with? Are they doing anything to take care of you as their team member? Or is their attitude one of, "you should just be grateful you have a job"?

How about the friend that wants you to ignore your nutrition plan so they don't feel guilty eating unhealthy food alone?

Even your children, yes your children, want to have power over you. They will cry, throw a tantrum, sulk and throw accusations of selfishness if you dare take care of yourself instead of seeing to their amusement.

I know many moms struggle with this but look at it from this perspective: one day your child will be a parent and they are learning from you how to treat themselves when they are a parent and what to expect of their partner as a parent. What are you modeling for them?

Self-care is your personal statement of worth. You, first and foremost, have to believe you are worthy of such care and attention.

If you have a hard time advocating for yourself, start here, by believing you are worthy of care and attention. When you start taking better care of yourself, you will begin to believe you deserve more. You will be less likely to settle or see yourself as less than anyone else.

Keep your self-care front and center so you can be at your best. Do you want more? A better life? Well, you've got to bring your A-game for that. Do you think you bring your A-game when you're tired, sluggish, overworked, and deprived of friend and family time?

No, you've got a C-game going — at best — under those conditions.

I'm just going to bottom line it. Taking care of you – body, mind, and soul – is the foundation of being *and* feeling successful.

People often dismiss this key component of success because they become overly focused on the end result — a new job, a career advancement, another degree or certification.

And, if you're in my tribe of entrepreneurial-minded, Type A, ambitious women, you know this is one of your stumbling blocks.

Success Starts with You

Anyone can push hard for an immediate goal. However, if your goal is for success that will last, you're going to have to take care of yourself.

Dr. Stephen Covey, author of the best-selling book *The 7 Habits of Highly Effective People,* calls it "Sharpen the Saw".

Successful people develop and maintain a balance or focus in four areas of life: physical, social/emotional, mental, and spiritual.

When we renew ourselves continually in each of these four areas, we enhance our ability to cope with the inevitable challenges that come at us.

Keep in mind that while self-care is key, it's imperative you pay close attention to your habits because your habits determine your success.

You can do all you want to take the best care of yourself — but if you're not willing to honestly examine *and* alter your habits — don't expect to get anywhere fast.

Here is a list of things that can proactively renew your energy; their opposites are the energy-stealers. I've broken them down into categories but, let me be clear, they all overlap.

Physical energy: sleep, good nutrition, exercise or activity, stretching, conscious breathing, and good hydration

Mental energy: keep life simple; minimize decision-making and make decisions in a timely manner; read books; watch videos; have conversations that stimulate your mind (TED talks are great for this); actively seek to communicate clearly to prevent confusion and ask that those around you do the same.

Emotional and spiritual energy: activities that bring you joy; spending time with happy, positive people; spending time with animals and being out in nature; being of service and taking time for reflection.

I'm going to focus on four key areas of self-care and there's also a worksheet below to help you identify where you need focus on taking better care of yourself.

Sleep It Off

Sleep is crucial because it not only contributes to your physical wellbeing, but also affects every area of your life.

How many hours of sleep do you need each night? Sleep isn't a one-size-fits-all thing.

No one knows your body better than you. You know what works for you – and what doesn't.

If you're not sure how many hours of sleep is best for you, experiment. Once you know your magic number, make sure you're getting it!

Get Up, Get Moving

Whether you're called to pound the pavement as a runner, put out some moves in kickboxing, or strike a pose in yoga, exercise is a great way to boost your energy and confidence. When you see what you're capable of physically, it can transform every other aspect of your life.

Pick a form of exercise that suits your personality.

Don't be discouraged if you really weren't into that Pilates session you tried out last week – keep trying different styles of exercise until you find the one that sends your pulse racing and keeps you coming back for more.

Jennifer Cohen, a Forbes.com contributor, named exercise as one of 5 things ultra-successful people do – before 8AM! Even if you're not an early riser, work with your own rhythm to keep things moving.

You Are What You Eat

Perhaps as important as sleep, eating well is another element of a healthy lifestyle.

Just like sleep isn't one-size-fits-all, you need to pay attention to what works for you, taking care to avoid foods that don't interact well with your body.

I recently took on a 30-day healthy eating plan, and I couldn't believe some of the changes I was seeing. I felt better not only in body, but I was also more focused, more energized and, yes, my clothes started fitting a little more loosely.

And while you're focused on healthy eating – don't leave out the H2O, which is essential to life itself. Even slight dehydration can impact your performance, causing fatigue, dizziness, reduced concentration, and decreased cognitive abilities.

Make Time, Take Time

Make time for activities that renew your soul – reading, hiking, time with friends, journaling, dancing, nature walks – even cleaning if that's what does it for you!

Taking time for yourself is a great way to avoid burnout and ultimately, boost productivity. Make downtime a *daily* ritual.

And don't forget about *alone time* – even if you think you're an extrovert. And that includes staying off email and any social media platforms.

Spending time alone can be a tough thing for many people, especially in our connected world, but it's necessary to allow your body and mind to recharge. Identify a couple areas to start with and make a plan to put more time for you and these activities into you schedule.

Now it's time to customize a plan to rejuvenate customized just for you.

Type this link into your browser to access the bonus materials: **womentakingthelead.com/resources**

In summation,

1. Have guarded time where you DO NOT WORK

2. Use this time to connect with yourself and the people in your personal life

3. Use this time for play and exploration

Taking these steps allows you to be in your feminine power to nurture and care for those around you without sacrificing your self-care.

PART II:
IT ALL BEGINS WITH YOU

"Set a goal so big that you can't achieve it, until you grow into the person who can." ~ Unknown

I'm here to help you grow into that person. I already see you that way.

Chapter 4:

Discovering Who You Are Starts with Determining Who You Are Not

"To know yourself as the Being underneath the thinker, the stillness underneath the mental noise, the love and joy underneath the pain, is freedom, salvation, enlightenment."

~Eckhart Tolle

I am a logical person and one of the most useful tools when applying logic is deduction — the process of ruling out. Deduction is very effective. So effective we call the ability to use it one's "powers of deduction."

You Are Not Your Former "Bad" Boss

In the workshops I do with young leaders I ask, "Who do you want to be as a leader?" They are often stumped by the question, but they quickly respond with, "I know who I don't want to be...my [current/former] bad boss."

That is the power of deduction.

We remember how we felt when we had to deal with someone who upset us, and it subconsciously shapes who we become as leader, a partner, a coworker, a friend, and a parent.

As a young leader, I put more thought into avoiding being perceived as a "bad boss" than I did in being a good boss. However, it led me to consider what experience I wanted to create for my team.

Here's one of my bad-boss stories:

At one point in my career in mutual fund operations, I was the team leader for the financial processing department. I inherited a new boss who came from another division.

This new boss was moved for several reasons. He was a friend of my department head, and he was starting to become a disruptive person in his previous role. It was thought that the change of scenery and new responsibilities would help him settle down, get serious, and shine as a new leader.

I'm sure you know where this is heading.

As the team leader of the financial department, I was accountable for our quality results and played the role of Quality Control. If mistakes were made, we were messing with other people's money and a lot of attention came down on us when any mistakes were made.

My new boss made hiring decisions based on a need to fill the seats, work experience, and, of course, friendship level. He did not hire for attitude or values... and before I knew it I was leading a team of 5 people — 4 of whom were on the disciplinary track for the *quality* of their work within 6 months!

One other person on the team should have been doing Quality Control with me for half their day but no one was qualified to do it — so I had to do it alone.

My new boss didn't feel comfortable with the task of Quality Control as he was new to the division, so he would give me a pep talk instead.

I was overwhelmed. I came in early, stayed late, and ate lunch at my desk to try to keep up with the work.

My boss came in on time, left on time, had lunch every day with his buddies and would spend parts of the day in his old division catching up with "old friends."

I gained 40 pounds in one year. I ate fast food to save time, I felt too tired to exercise, and I starting drinking wine at the end of the day to assist in letting the stress go. I had never been much of a drinker before this point.

Then came my opportunity to be promoted to Supervisor, move to Maine, and develop a whole new team.

Can you imagine the type of leader I committed to be for this new team?

My team over the next 8 years would describe me as hands-on, supportive, caring, dedicated, focused, quality-driven, and hard working.

I never wanted anyone who worked for me to feel like I felt working for my former boss. And to my knowledge no one did.

Starting from a place of who I was not as a leader, I came to an identity of who I am as a leader.

Now leadership aside, let's get at who you are not *as a person*.

You Are Not Your Stress Reactions

Have you ever been in a negative relationship or a situation and over time you notice there are some changes in your personality and how you respond to things? Changes and responses that you're not proud of?

The television dramas would say, "He makes me a better person," or, "She makes me want to be a better person." In reality, you find yourself uttering, "I don't like the person I am when I'm around them," or, "When I'm there, I'm like a different person."

This is *who you are not!*

You say those things and you do those things... but they feel wrong, and you don't like it. That's the sign that it's not THE REAL YOU operating in these situations.

Whenever you feel at odds with how you are showing up and how you are behaving, you are sure to find your default stress reaction at play. This is your alter ego, the persona you become under stress to try to protect you from any perceived threat.

When I get stressed, I become very controlling. I micromanage and get lost in details and research. If you know me, you would know details and research are not where I choose to hang out on a day-to-day basis.

Likely, when your alter ego is at play, you'll find yourself doing things that are the opposite of what you would normally do if things weren't so tense.

The issue with the alter ego is it started to develop when you were very young, when you didn't know as much as you do now. Think 6-8 years old.

e the alter ego first came into existence, you have become more experienced, skilled, wise and resourceful. But your alter ego isn't aware of that and so it jumps in to save the day thinking you are not capable to handle the situation and that you are still 8 years old. Instead of saving the day, your alter ego makes you feel small, incapable and out of control.

By going over some common stress reactions, I'm hoping you will gain an awareness of your own alter ego so you'll be able to see it in action when something stressful occurs. With this awareness, you'll be able to make a different choice; you'll be able to respond to stress as you really are: powerful, capable, resourceful and committed.

Type this link into your browser to access the bonus materials that go along with each of the stress reactions: **womentakingthelead.com/resources**

1. Shutting down: Cocooning

Imagine you are going about your day when suddenly, something happens.

No matter what it is, it *occurs* to you as bad news. The worst news. The last thing you needed right now. The straw that broke the camel's back. It could be a change to your carefully laid out plans, an unpleasant conversation, a flat tire, burnt toast... whatever.

It really doesn't matter. What matters is that it's something you don't like, and you feel like it's **out of your control**.

And then you feel the energy drain out of your body. You're tired and defeated, and you start to wonder why you try so hard. It's already X o'clock, and you feel like you need a nap.

But you can't take a nap, so instead you go in your office and close the door, or you go to your phone to see what's happening on Facebook, or you get in your car to go to Starbucks to get a jolt of caffeine. If you're at home, you sit on the couch and do a Netflix marathon.

You. Are. Shutdown. Your batteries became depleted, and you are now doing anything you can to recharge.

You may also be in a mindset where you can't stand to be around yourself and nothing makes you happy. You may feel ashamed of yourself, worthless.

You can't stand to have people see you like this, so you hide out and **go into your cocoon.** You isolate yourself from others and keep them at a distance.

This is not *YOU*.

This is your alter ego in survival mode. It will help you to recover, but it's not the most effective way to hit your goals or to achieve the life you want to live. While you may be recovering, you are falling a little further behind on your goals and you are ineffective at anything you try to do.

The real you is effective, capable and resourceful, but that persona has taken a back seat and given the power to the alter ego.

Warning: Do not make decisions when the alter ego is in charge. They will be decisions made from the perspective of an 8 year old. What does an 8 year old know about what you are capable of? Exactly. Don't give your alter ego decision-making power.

The key here is to be aware that the alter ego has taken over. When you are aware, the power is back in your court and you can make a different decision if you'd like. This is important to note. You are always powerful and in every situation you have a choice. We often experience stress because we have convinced ourselves that we have no power in the situation, that everything is being done to us, and we just have to take it.

It's not true. For whatever reason, in that situation you have decided to abdicate your power to your alter ego (probably because the choice is a difficult one) but you always have your personal power to choose your attitude and your behavior.

You can choose to see the situation differently and see where you do have power and control — where the woman of your experience and skill can make a difference.

There are times when I let that controlling part of myself off the leash so I can dive into the details and research the dickens out of a certain topic. But I'm doing it by choice and not because I feel out of control. I use my default stress reaction to serve me and not the other way around.

Life is duality. You are both in control and powerless. The key is to be in control when you are in control and to let things unfold when you are not in control... and dare I say, enjoy the ride?

2. Overreacting: The Amazon Warrior

Similar to the situation above, something happens but in this instance your alter ego's faulty radar picks up something different. Rather than sensing a situation where there is nothing you can do, your alter ego picks up a threat.

That change to your carefully laid out plans, the unpleasant conversation, the flat tire, the burnt toast — they are now perceived as putting something at risk, something important. This creates **conflict**.

The alter ego is now charged up and ready to battle! Rather than turning into the Incredible Hulk (we're women, after all) you become *The Amazon Warrior*.

Being an Amazon Warrior might sound eccentric and sexy. But no one likes to be around this woman and this woman fights for everything that she wants. She's so unpleasant that people only help her if they think they have to.

The battle that you create in this stress reaction can come in the following forms:

1. Aggression: verbal and/or physical (though likely at your age, you redirect physical aggression into some sort of workout)

2. Passive-aggression

3. Fuming silently

4. Perfectionism

5. Jealousy ("the more they get, the less I get")

6. Second-guessing yourself (yup, this battle is with you)

This stress reaction has more energy than the reaction of shutting down so you're unlikely to find yourself lying on the couch, at least not right away. But this burst of energy is on credit and you pay it back with interest. Once the adrenaline rush has passed, you will likely find yourself in need of some recovery time.

Also, when your alter ego is in charge of this stress reaction, the actions you take will be misdirected, get you a result that is only temporary, and land you with consequences that may be worse than the original threat.

This stress reaction causes us to say things we don't mean (to ourselves and others), take our fear and anger out on innocent bystanders, and make snap-decisions in the heat of the moment.

Even if you are somewhat aware of your internal conflict, your attempt to hide it is futile. You'll find yourself being critical of yourself and others, you'll involuntarily focus on the negative (threats!) and your tone of voice/word choice/body language will give you away.

A coach of mine called this *leaking.* It's gross but accurate.

You are trying to hide your volatile mood, but it leaks out and, as a consequence, you occur to other people as "not quite right."

This is not *YOU*.

This is your alter ego on high alert, looking for threats, and trying to protect you. It is defensive, augmentative and just waiting for someone to say or do that "thing" and it will lash out.

Again, to gain control over your alter ego awareness is key. Be aware of what is pushing your buttons: what feels threatened and what is causing the threat?

Realize that a large percentage of the threats you perceive are just that, *perceived threats.* They are not real and if you can stay in reality, you can keep yourself from turning into The Amazon Warrior.

Lastly, and I don't say this lightly, stay away from gossip, complainers, negativity and workplace drama — this will create inner conflict and pull you into attitudes and behaviors that are NOT YOU.

3. Tolerating/Coping: The Chameleon

While this stress reaction is much more agreeable and feels better than shutting down or over-reacting, if you constantly choose this method of dealing with stress you will never be truly happy. This is the stress reaction of choosing your battles but you must choose wisely.

While tolerating and coping are great short-term strategies they are debilitating long-term strategies.

For example, if you had guests coming for the weekend, you're not likely to bring up and address every little thing they do that doesn't follow house rules or just plain gets on your nerves. They are there for a short time and the goal is to make your guests comfortable and for everyone to have a good time.

So, you tell yourself they just don't know better, you put it aside and move on.

However, if these guests were building a new home and out of the graciousness of your heart you offered to have them live with you for 3-6 months, it would be a different story. In this instance you would be better off using a different strategy: having a conversation up front about house rules, expectations and strategies of dealing with conflict.

But many of us don't think to set expectations in advance. You see, we have been raised to be ***The Chameleon***.

We grew up hearing, "If you don't have anything nice to say don't say anything at all," or "Bite your tongue."

Instead of resolving conflict, we stew in silence or vent to a trusted friend and colleague. Venting relieves some of the pressure but the problem remains.

In the wild, chameleons are known for their ability to blend into their environment. They take on the colors and patterns around them so a predator cannot detect their presence.

The problem is when you become the chameleon, you hide who you really are and take on a persona that feels uncomfortable to you. And, it takes a tremendous amount of energy for you to change your spots, so to speak. More energy than you realize.

Think about when you come into a new situation and you're meeting new people. You're likely on your "best behavior" because you want to make a good impression or at the very least not make a bad impression. You put extra effort into your appearance, think about what you say before you say it, and your behavior is guided by what's proper or expected.

How exhausted are you by the time you're back in your home, your safe space, and you can let your guard down?

Now consider all the areas, relationships, and places in your life where you overlook and tolerate things that bother you simply because you "don't want to make a fuss". You've adapted to these situations over time. They aren't flashbulb, sudden events. You likely don't even give much conscious thought to them anymore — but your subconscious is giving them a lot of consideration.

In relationships, are you being nice (inauthentic) or are you being kind (compassionate)? Because sometimes compassion looks like telling someone the truth, even if it causes conflict, even if they don't want to hear it, and even if you don't want to say it.

Sometimes telling someone "it's fine" when it's not is a betrayal to the relationship. Non-conflict becomes more important than the relationship.

Is it truly not a big deal or is the truth that you are too uncomfortable with conflict so you'll be miserable rather than say anything?

This is all well and dandy until one day, these little situations become "threatening" to your lifelong happiness and The Amazon Warrior comes out.

Our alter ego tricks us into believing "non-conflict" is the same as peace and harmony. But it's a lie. Because the conflict still lives within you and there is a price to pay when you wage that war on the inside.

If you feel tired in the morning, have a hard time focusing on or engaging in what's in front of you, or you need to recover on the weekends, you are likely using this stress reaction as a coping strategy in your life.

Many people use "I'm getting old" to dismiss the symptoms of this stress reaction but that's just denial. That's The Chameleon at play. Take "I'm getting old" out of your vocabulary and replace it with "I'm not dealing with something."

The devastating effects of using this stress reaction as a long-term strategy are the same effects of growing old quickly. I know many people who feel and act like they are 20 years older than their real age. The tolerating is taking a toll on their body.

There is a cure for this mysterious early-aging disease. It's called conflict resolution.

When my clients go through my coaching system, they identify everything they are tolerating in their lives and start addressing them one-by-one. In no time they start feeling different.

I often hear:

"I feel like a weight has been lifted."

"I never noticed how hard it was to breathe but after the conversations I started taking deeper breaths. I had no idea."

"I cleaned out the garage this weekend. I have no idea where the energy came from."

Have you ever wondered where some people get the energy they have? If you take a close look, you'll probably see a person who addresses conflict calmly and directly as it arises. They are not using The Chameleon as their stress reaction, so they don't waste energy on being someone they are not.

Is it time for you to let go of being The Chameleon?

To prevent The Chameleon's energy drain, commit to being true to who you are and what you are feeling. Say "no" when you want to say "no". Say "yes" when you want to say "yes."

If it's a situation that requires you to make a sacrifice to honor your values, give up feeling like it's a sacrifice by choosing it 100%. If you're going to say yes anyway, do it wholeheartedly. It's feeling like it's an obligation that's messing with your energy.

If you're interested in identifying all the areas of toleration in your life, I've got a worksheet that can help you with that.

4. Focusing on Others: Superhero Syndrome

Oh, how I love to help others. It makes me feel so good to solve other people's problems, give them a helping hand, and take some of the stress off their shoulders.

I especially love it when I don't want to deal with my own projects and problems.

Being able to focus on someone else for a while takes the attention off what's causing me stress in my own life. This is a sure-fire way for me to feel better for a little while.

The problem is, while I'm off saving the day for someone else, my own stuff gets neglected: my business, my home, my finances, my health, etc.

All you current and recovering people-pleasers, are you with me?!

Tell me if this sounds familiar: It starts as you giving out of the generosity of our own heart. You see a need that you know you can take care of and your instinct is to take care of it. Because that's you, you're a giving person. It's part of your identity.

So you swoop in and contribute your time, energy, and/or resources, and it is so appreciated that you light up on the inside. It's like a drug. You get a jolt of the feel-goods, so you do it again. And it starts to become a regular thing. So regular that other people stop relating to it as a gift that you generously, and with sacrifice to your own needs, give — and they start taking it for granted.

Now it's no longer a gift, it's an obligation, and obligations don't make you feel good, they make you feel burdened. But if you stopped giving, people would wonder what's wrong with you, what made you so upset. And that's not you. You're not the type of person that takes things away just because you're upset. That's childish, and you're not childish.

This is now a crisis to your identity. Continue to give resentfully or take it away and risk your reputation as a helpful, giving, and generous person? Now you are on the hunt for any semi-valid excuse for why you can no longer give what's expected of you.

I mean, you can't possible just come out and say it no longer works for you to give or heaven forbid... ask to be recognized and appreciated for what you give. Heavens to Betsy, *who the hell does that?!*

All the while, your own needs, your projects, and your mission in life take a back seat — only to be given attention when there are deadlines, emergencies or wake-up calls.

And the saga continues. Cue the music.

Or maybe this is your wake-up call. Maybe it's time to look at what you need and what you want and start seeing that your needs and wants are met.

This is The Superhero Syndrome.

Another aspect of this syndrome is the constant need to fix problems, save the day and be the hero.

Helping someone find solutions and helping them resolve a problem when they want and need your help is great, but with The Superhero Syndrome help is given even if it is not asked for and, sometimes, when it isn't needed. The Superhero will become frustrated if others won't let them help because The Superhero believes they know better.

Like allowing a toddler to wobble and fall as they are beginning to walk, we all need space to make mistakes and learn by doing. Now imagine The Superhero swooping in whenever the toddler goes to stand and takes their hand. That toddler will take a lot longer to learn to walk because they won't develop the proper muscles or come to understand balance as quickly.

The Superhero sees people in need like toddlers about to fall and hit their head on the coffee table. It's done with love and care but, with this perception, The Superhero has put themselves above everyone else. Without knowing it The Superhero sends a message to others that The Superhero is better than them.

If you find yourself suffering from The Superhero Syndrome, you are likely exhausted trying to keep everyone else from falling apart or making bad decisions. You also don't have the time you'd like to get your own house in order.

You're so busy taking care of everyone else your life has taken a back seat.

But if you want to have the life you envisioned, you have to switch from being the fixer to being the mentor (if that's what the other person wants you to be).

To make sure your generosity and giving continue to feel good and a source of renewing energy for you, start setting boundaries around your giving. Only give when you choose it, when it works for you.

If giving feels like an obligation, either try to recreate it so there's some energy there, or if it is no longer something that draws you, bring it to an end in a way that works for you and your values.

Really consider what you want and what you need. Do you know what you need and what you want – and the difference between the two?

onsider what works for you and what does not for you. There might be some uncomfortable conversations to be had but consider how uncomfortable it's going to be for you to continue doing something that doesn't work for you.

By being true to ourselves, we model for others how they can be true to themselves as well.

Managing Your Alter Ego

If it helps you to name your alter ego, draw it, journal about it, or write a song about it... do it! The more aware you are of this part of you, the more control you will have over it.

When you know the thoughts, feelings and behaviors you have — and the things that trigger them — when your alter ego has taken over, you will be better at catching it before it has done too much damage.

Trust me, knowing is half the battle. You are going to feel like a whole new woman as you start working through this process.

If you want help identifying your stress reactions, I have an assessment that I use with my clients. It gets to the heart of the stress reactions that are running their show and keeping them from hitting their goals.

Go here to find out more: **womentakingthelead.com/assessment**

You Are Not Your Self-Imposed Limiting Story

I don't think it will come as a surprise for anyone that in the past year I've spent a lot of time contemplating our position as women in the workplace, in the home, and in society — more than I ever have in the past.

Multiple conversations per week flow into more conversations and more pondering. Sometimes, I admit, I get a little overwhelmed — like I'm trying to crack a code that no one has been able to solve yet.

There are many reasons why, as women, we are faced with bias and some are out of our control.

However, I've come to see the biggest obstacle to our confidence and equal opportunities is ourselves.

Collectively, it is our own self-imposed limits that are having the greatest impact on the slow progress we've had as women.

Stay with me for a bit:

In grammar school, my peers and I were assigned in work groups based on what our ability was believed to be in certain subjects and the teacher taught each group according to our perceived ability.

When I was in the third grade, I was placed in the middle reading group in school. At some point during the year, my teacher met with my parents to propose moving me to the higher reading group because the workload in my level was too easy for me.

The change was made and the problems began.

I wasn't finishing my work, and it wasn't at the same caliber it had been.

My peaceful existence in the third grade suddenly changed. I was publicly ridiculed by my teacher and accused of being lazy. My teacher seemed to look for opportunities to criticize me.

In the third grade, I began wetting myself at school.

Luckily in the fourth grade, I had a wonderful and compassionate teacher, and I worked hard to prove myself worthy of her kindness. I excelled in school through the sixth grade and was always in the top groups.

Then when transitioning to Catholic school in the seventh grade, I tested into the middle level.

I was shocked by the results, since I'd been in the top levels since third grade but it was explained to me that Catholic school was harder than public school, and I was actually an average student in this new system. I wasn't happy, but I accepted what I was told.

Until high school, when I tested into the highest level once again. At an older age with firmer beliefs, after two years of believing myself an average student, I could not accept this change.

My parents were pleased but I was not. I was freaked out. Remember the last experience I had when moved into a higher level?

The thought that ran through my head as I sat in the classroom on the first day of school was, "I don't belong here. I don't belong here. I'm going to fail."

This was reinforced when a girl from my previous school, who had been in a higher level, looked at me with surprise as she walked into the room that first day and asked what I was doing there.

I transferred this thought to my new classmates in the room. It didn't matter that they didn't know me. In my mind, they knew I was a fraud and that I shouldn't be there.

For weeks, I begged, I pleaded, and I lashed out in anger at my parents and my guidance counselor. They wouldn't budge. I had tested well, and I belonged in the honors level classes. In their mind — that was that, case closed.

Long story short, I intentionally flunked Biology that first quarter and my parents and guidance counselor, much to their chagrin, agreed to move me down two levels to the middle level.

Do you know it took me the next 2½ years to get back into honors level classes? The reality was that I didn't belong in the middle level classes.

It was only after meeting an amazing teacher who helped me begin to change the beliefs about my abilities (and it was reinforced by other teachers around me) that I could see that I had been wrong about myself.

Until I changed my belief that I was only an average student, I couldn't excel in school.

This isn't just the case with me, this happens to us all.

We create an outward reality that reflects the internal beliefs we have. The two have to connect.

This is the crux of the work I do with my clients.

When they change their limiting beliefs about themselves and what's possible, they suddenly have a renewed energy and confidence to take action.

With these new actions, things start to change, and they start getting the things they've always wanted but couldn't seem to make a reality... be it better relationships, more money, or to finally write their book.

Until we as women are willing to believe that we are worthy of more, that we deserve the right to speak up and advocate for ourselves and to be treated well — what we will get is what we've always gotten.

Isn't it time you got something different?

I saw a meme on Facebook recently that stated, "When you stand up for yourself as a woman you stand up for all women."

I couldn't deny the truth in the statement.

What are some of the self-imposed limiting stories you need to let go of?

Type this link into your browser to access the bonus materials: **womentakingthelead.com/resources**

Chapter 5:

Getting to Know the Real You

"Find out who you are and be that person. That's what your soul was put on this Earth to be. Find that truth, live that truth and everything else will come."

~ Ellen DeGeneres

Now that you know who you don't want to be and who you aren't let's get to who you really are.

A good place to start is your values. Your values are at the core of who you are. Without thought, your values guide you through your day-to-day life. You know your values have been honored when you feel really great about something you did or a decision you made.

And guess what? You will also know when you, or someone else, has dishonored one of your values. You will immediately become upset.

In her book, Fierce Conversations, Susan Scott addressed the field of Pscho-neuro-immunology and the studies that point out that the strength of our immune system is directly related to how closely we live by our values.

We actually strengthen our immune system by honoring our values. Since we do not intentionally dishonor our values we may not be aware of the consequences until we start feeling the symptoms of exhaustion, lethargy, and discontent.

Whenever something bothers me, I quickly do what I call a "Values Scan" to see which value(s) have been infringed upon. Once I have that awareness, I do what's in my power to put it right.

You do not want to achieve success while dishonoring your values. Those who try usually sacrifice their health to do so.

Think of people who go to work every day to a job they hate. They know something is wrong, but they convince themselves they don't have a choice in the matter. So they start overeating or drinking, or gambling or... fill in the blank.

Chronic disease is also prevalent among those that know their life is not on track. Do you have any idea how many clients I have who have arthritis, chronic fatigue syndrome, fibromyalgia or some other debilitating condition?

Their body has been screaming at them for years, but the good news is they are doing something about it now. Uncovering what their values are, and honoring those values as a priority, alleviates some of the suffering.

Are you ready to get at your core values?

Type this link into your browser to access the bonus materials: **womentakingthelead.com/resources**

Now that you know what your values are, and who you are at your core, you can use them to guide you in any decision you need to make. Whenever you are faced with a new decision, ask yourself, what choice will honor my highest values?

Identify Your Superpowers

I've talked **before** about how we're entering an era where success in business will be determined by the relationships we've built over time.

As a leader, what does this mean for you? A lot.

Today, many employees value the overall culture of an organization, the amount of freedom they'll have in their position, and how they can contribute to and make an impact there.

Consumers aren't basing their buying choices solely on cost. They're researching before making a purchase to find out what a brand *really* represents – its mission, values, and history.

Given this shift, strong leadership itself is a superpower. And our society is ever obsessed with superhero figures.

When I was a child I wanted to be like Wonder Woman, She-Ra, and GI Jane.

In my years as a corporate leader, I loved the more recent superhero characters in Trinity from The Matrix, Lara Croft from Tomb Raider, and Michelle Yeoh's character from Crouching Tiger Hidden Dragon.

To me, these characters embodied strength, self-assurance, and a willingness to take a different path. They endeavored for the greater good at great sacrifice to themselves. I found inspiration in their stories.

They had superb fighting skills but used them judiciously and only when necessary.

Defining Your Leadership Superpowers

As a leader, take a moment to reflect on your **own** superpowers — those special qualities that make you shine in your role.

Here are some qualities that come to mind when I think of leadership superpowers:

1. Authenticity: You say what you mean, and mean what you say. You consider whether your actions are really aligned with your inner thoughts and feelings. You're not afraid to speak up when something needs to be said.

2. Reliability: Others can count on you. Sure, we all make mistakes from time to time – but you own up to yours and work to make it right. Everyone knows you're dependable and won't jump ship when the going gets tough.

3. Inspiration: You bring out the best in others, encouraging them to discover – and use – their own superpowers. People are motivated not only by your own unique strengths, but also by your ability to hone in on theirs.

Other superpowers I think of are: warmth, humor, being open to constructive feedback, sharing (judiciously) your thoughts and personal stories, visionary thinking, listening, the ability to plan effectively and to successfully re-route those plans when they don't fall into place, willingness to commit, and a desire to give back to others.

Use Those Superpowers!

Just like your favorite superhero, use your superpowers to build quality relationships, lead your team, and inspire others – in business and in life.

Remember, nearly every professional interaction gives you the opportunity to build – or slowly destroy – your relationships.

And as any great superhero would, wield your powers to annihilate any quality (we all have them!) that isn't serving your highest good: being overly judgmental, critical, or condescending, blaming others, being argumentative or continually wanting to prove your point, or even being unresponsive.

And, since you're only human, after all, when you need a little inspiration of your own, just envision your favorite superhero, busting through all that evil and making everything all right again...

Here are some other indicators you can use to get to know yourself better and identify your unique Superpowers:

1. DiSC

2. Myers Briggs

3. Strength finders

4. Fascination Advantage

There are many more indicators but these are the more popular ones and the ones I am most familiar with. If you have another you are more familiar with, take that one. The point is to seek clarity around what makes you tick so that you can use this knowledge to your advantage.

When I found out two of my strengths were enthusiasm and collaboration I was not completely surprised. Looking back on my career, I could see how those traits helped me to stand out of the crowd.

However, with the awareness that these traits make me stand out, I can plan my business activities around these traits... and avoid situations where I am weakest.

Activities that Are Your Kryptonite

If we are talking about your strengths, we are going to need to talk about your weaknesses. Those areas that take much more of your focus and attention (to only be half as good as the areas of your strengths) are clearly your weaknesses.

These are the abilities that don't come naturally to you.

Is it worth expending a lot of energy improving your weaknesses? That is a topic long debated.

My opinion is that if it will benefit you to improve an area you are weak in then do it. If you're doing it as a hobby, great.

If you're expending a good chunk of your resources (time, money, energy) on trying to go from a 3 out of 10 to a 5 out of 10, I say outsource whatever that ability is for you and save your energy on activities that will have a greater impact for you.

For instance, I outsource any technical updates of my website and Search Engine Optimization (SEO). Could I spend an entire weekend or more learning how to do this myself? Sure. But I would hate it, and I would be wrecked for the rest of the week.

I'll also be hiring someone to edit this book. Right now I'm data-dumping everything I know on the page, adding in my personal experience with these concepts and ordering it all in a way that makes sense.

But details and dealing with minutia are not my strengths. It would be draining for me. I would quickly get distracted and soon I would find more important things that need my attention, even though I know that is not true!

Truth gets blurry when we are overcome by our kryptonite. Deadlines get missed and before I know it, two months will have passed and this drafted book would sit, unedited and unpublished.

No, for the last stage, I will have someone else weed through all of the material and polish a finished product.

Type this link into your browser to access the bonus materials: **womentakingthelead.com/resources**

Chapter 6:

Your Personal Mission

(Your "Why")

"When the why is clear, the how is easy."

~Unknown

When I was a young girl, I knew in my gut that God had put me on the Earth to do something special. I heard the bible stories, and I knew that, some day, I would have a dream in which God or an angel would speak to me and tell me what my special mission was.

These were the stories I grew up with. The Old Testament is full of them. God was constantly talking to people. I couldn't wait!

And then, as I got a little older, another element of these stories appeared. These stories didn't always have happy endings.

In fact, the ones who didn't die a horrible death usually didn't live a great life either. Poor Moses was kept out of The Promised Land after all he went through.

Now being called on by God didn't seem so great anymore. I prayed one night for God NOT to call on me. I asked to live an ordinary life.

And for a time I had my way. My life was an ordinary life, and I did ordinary things. In college and throughout my 20s, I envied those people who knew exactly what they were meant to be doing. All the while, I still had this growing feeling in me that I was meant for more, that I should be doing more, and that I was throwing my life away to live an ordinary existence.

This feeling began to plague me after I received my final promotion in my corporate job. I started in Mutual Fund Operations in June of 2000, and, by December of 2005, I was offered my 5th promotion as the Assistant Vice

President of Corporate Quality. I was shocked and overjoyed to be trusted so much (and a little nervous for the upcoming changes and added responsibilities).

I went at this new role with gusto. I was determined to prove that it was not a mistake and the right person had been chosen for the job. After 6-9 months of furious activity, everything started to settle down, and I was left with a lot of time to think.

I considered the lifestyles of those above me. The Vice Presidents of my company were working long hours. They would call in from their vacations to be on conference calls that anyone from their division could have covered.

They seemed to be tethered to work and the idea chafed at my need for freedom.

Knowing I wasn't really looking for that 6th promotion, but happy in my current role, I was left with time for reflection. It was the perfect formula for growing discontent.

Soon I found myself staring out the window wondering, "Is this it? Is this all I'm meant to do?"

Or, a little voice piped up, could I be doing more of what I enjoyed doing: inspiring and motivating people to bring forth their best in a bigger arena?

During this time, I was introduced to a couple of professional life and business coaches at a backyard barbecue, and I instantly became intrigued. They were cheerful, they listened intently, and they asked great questions.

They stood out to me because, frankly, at a party where a lot is going on and people are drinking, how often to you have someone's FULL attention for more than a minute at a time?

There was something about them that I admired, and I needed to find out more. I began my research.

I talked to more coaches and researched certification programs. That part seemed straight forward, but what wasn't so clear to me was how they found clients and made money. OK, I'll be honest; it *was* clear how they found clients and made money- sales, ugh! I didn't like that answer, so I kept looking for the answer I wanted, but I didn't find it.

Only once in my life have I ever had to do a big job search and that one time was stressful enough. ("You mean to tell me I would have to search for work over and over and over again? I would now be in *Sales???*")

While I was AVP, the economy took a downturn after the real estate crash, and I started to get nervous.

Clink!

That's the sound of the Golden Handcuffs making their presence known.

The Golden Handcuffs is a term used to describe a situation in which you are so well compensated that you're willing to be unhappy to keep it.

I was appreciated, respected, and well paid in my current job. The only problem was that I wasn't satisfied or fulfilled in my job, and I wanted to be a professional coach.

I slowly grew bored and discontent. I distracted myself with fitness, travel, and dating — anything to keep my attention off how I felt about my career.

And then the Universe intervened with what felt like two car crashes. No, I didn't get into any car accidents, but I did live through two mergers and acquisitions.

If you've never been through an acquisition or a divorce, it would be hard to describe the upheaval, uncertainty of the future, and the sweeping and unsettling changes that come through your world.

It doesn't just affect you: Every person that you spend the majority of your waking hours with is also going through emotional upheaval as well. It's both comforting and a burden. Everyone is on their own emotional roller coaster but your peaks and valleys aren't in sync... they come at different times. On days where you felt better (or more in control), you were sure to encounter several people who were freaking out. When you were freaking out, you were sure to encounter those who seemed to be aloof to the situation.

We were all in it together but we were not having the same experience.

During this crazy time, someone recommended to me Eckhart Tolle's book, *A New Earth*.

Right from the beginning, this book gripped me. The story of how flowers evolved, an analogy of the awakening of a whole new level of human consciousness, was that dream from God that I imagined I would have as a child. I wasn't sleeping, but the message was clear: I was meant to guide people to a new level of consciousness and self-awareness.... to bring about a new earth, one they hadn't experienced before.

I was on fire. This was my calling. I didn't know exactly what it was going to look like, but I was certain I could no longer settle for the half life that I was currently living.

I did what I would ask any of my clients to do, I took those first few baby steps.

Now it's your turn to consider your life purpose. You may not have had a light bulb moment like mine (yet, anyway) but, chances are, if you've been paying attention, you have had experiences that can point you in the direction of your personal mission.

The following exercise was shared with me during my coach certification program and was attributed to Tony Robbin's "Date with Destiny" program.

Type this link into your browser to access the bonus materials: **womentakingthelead.com/resources**

Whenever I read my personal mission statement and the mission of Women Taking the Lead, it still brings me back to that epiphany I had when I began reading *A New Earth*.

My Personal Mission Statement:

I, Jodi-Marie Flynn, *hear*, *see*, *feel* and *know* that the purpose of my life is to be a vibrantly expressed, playful adventurer; to enjoy, create and celebrate the abundance and wisdom of the universe and to love, nurture and strengthen myself and others.

Mission of the Women Taking the Lead Podcast:

Women Taking the Lead is dedicated to joining forces with women and men to foster the development of women as leaders. By helping girls and women to overcome conditioning and self-doubt and to see that their gifts and talents are so valuable that they are compelled to contribute, we are creating a more prosperous and peaceful world.

For this next exercise, I want you to relax and give yourself permission to have whatever you want, not what everyone else wants. What *you* really want. If you struggle with this, then put it on me. I give you permission to have what you want.

If you were living your personal mission statement... the one you created above, what would your ideal day look like? Start with waking up and end with going to sleep. What do you do during the day, who do you interact with and how do you *feel* about it?

Take some time to write it out.

Type this link into your browser to access the bonus materials: **womentakingthelead.com/resources**

When you've completed your Ideal Day, stretch it out to the week. You don't have to include as many details as you did for the entire day, but what are some of the other activities and people you would include if you could stretch it to an entire Ideal Week? Again, give yourself permission to have whatever you want. If it helps, I give you permission to have what you want.

Affirmations

Now I want you to take elements of that ideal day and week to create some affirmations.

I know, I know. If you're one of my logical, left-brained, Type-A women I know the word "affirmations" is likely causing you to roll your eyes.

Stay with me and think of it this way: affirmations are reminders. They are statements designed to impact your conscious and unconscious thought patterns. Affirmations are "truth" statements that you forgot.

They are always said in the present tense and are positive. You will not see any of the following language in an affirmation:

"One day..."

"Once X then..."

"does not"

"won't"

"not"

"no"

"will not"

If you find yourself projecting into the future, state it as if it is already happening. If you find yourself using a negative word change it to a positive. For example,

Futuristic and negative: "One day I won't have a boss anymore."

Present and positive: "I am the CEO of my brand."

It doesn't matter if it is "true" currently. Think and live like it is already true. Affirmations disrupt your brain patterns and, with practice, your conscious and subconscious mind will accept it as reality and you will live like it is true. And when you live like it is true, your energy is focused on attaining that goal.

These statements will *reaffirm* what you already know from your Ideal Day and Ideal Week.

Here are some affirmations, that I repeat to myself to focus my personal power.

I am divinely guided.

I change the world for the better with every conversation I have.

Money flows to me easily and effortlessly.

I am surrounded by opportunities.

I am loved and supported in my mission.

Now you try it. On a separate piece of paper write down at least 5-10 affirmations that support your Ideal Day and Week.

Type this link into your browser to access the bonus materials: **womentakingthelead.com/resources**

Repeat these affirmations in the morning and at night and, when they become more familiar, throughout the day.

Between your commitment to self-care, consciously choosing your stress reaction, and bringing the real you forward with awareness — you're going to start showing up in your life very powerfully.

I'll venture to say you'll be damn near unstoppable.

Chapter 7:

The People Who Surround You

"Show Me Your Friends and I'll Show You Your Future."

~ Chaplain Ronnie Melancon

"You are the average of the five people you spend the most time with."

~ Jim Rohn

Do we really follow the exact same path as our friends? No, I don't believe that.

But I do believe we are tethered to our friends. If we are more successful than our closest friends, it will only be by a margin.

And if we are not as successful as our friends, it will only be by a margin as well.

The reason for this is that we start to absorb the messages our friends send and soon they become our messages and vice versa. If your friends have a negative mentality, your positive mentality will impact them and lift them up but what will you be absorbing in the mean time?

Grab a piece of paper and make a list of those in your life whom:

1. You need to boost yourself up before seeing

2. Are always complaining

3. When things are going well, they are looking for and pointing out the negative

4. Talk mostly about themselves

5. If they ask about you, they get distracted before you are done and/or immediately turn the conversation back to them

6. Leave you feeling drained

82

You also have to be careful of those who want to be around your positivity because it temporarily makes them feel better but they have no commitment to change. They will take your energy and will not reciprocate anything but their crankiness and dark thoughts.

I want to underscore that these behaviors are the result of powerful alter egos. These individuals are under stress and are acting in the best way they know how to deal with it. Please have tremendous compassion for them and encourage them to get help if you are close to someone like this and it's appropriate, but do not allow your Superhero Syndrome alter ego take over to try to "fix" them yourself.

Here are some examples so you can identify these toxic personas and steer clear.

The Martyr

Not to be confused with The Superhero who is going above and beyond to take care of everyone else, this martyr gives very little and expects the world to take care of them.

They often expound upon all the things in their life that have gone wrong, are unfair, and no one else has had to deal with. Many people have divorced parents but the martyr will have details outlining why their parent's divorce was worse than what anyone else had to deal with. And it compounds.

The divorce led to them moving around a lot, which led to them not having a lot of close friends growing up, which led to dating a lot of losers which led... you get the picture.

When something bad happens, they knew it was going to happen. When something good happens, they have a snarky comment for that too.

I became friends with a girl-woman in college who in the stage of getting-to-know-you seemed calm and cheerful. I liked that.

But over time, I noticed she would dwell on things that did not go her way. She rolled her eyes and sighed a lot. She had a dramatic story about her childhood, and I sympathized with her about that, her classes, her current friends and so on.

Instead of becoming cheerful once again after venting, she would stay stuck being sad and discontent. I started noticing that I would hesitate before calling her or knocking on her door.

One day she was crying in an unconvincing way because she had just had an argument with her mom (for the 50th time), and I realized I didn't feel anything. I was dried up. I had nothing left to give. And I was becoming sad too.

Now realizing this was way beyond anything I could help, I suggested she see the counselor on campus (only to find out she hated the counselor). I named several other people on campus only to have each one shot down.

She was content to have things go on as they were, but I was not. I slowly phased out that friendship. I called less, visited less, had less availability, and soon she found other friends.

There are pastors and counselors that help those with a negative mindset, but they are highly trained to do that specific work. Unless you are also highly trained for this work (and keep in mind friendship blurs this training as well), you are likely not able to help them. Or as in my case, you may make them worse by becoming a co-dependent, giving away your energy to them.

Suggest they seek help and support them in finding a trained support system, but do not let them continually drain your precious energy.

Sometimes love looks like tough love.

The Gossip

When I started my job in Mutual Fund Operations it was the first time I worked in cubicle land. Having studied and trained for counseling, I never imagined that would be my work environment. I imagined most of my days spent having one-to-one conversations and maybe, on occasion, doing some group work.

But here I was sitting in my cubicle, excited for the opportunity and wanting to do a good job.

The woman who sat visibly across from me was a woman in her 50s, and she was warm and friendly when I started. She worked in a different department doing different work, but she would give me information that would be helpful to me.

And as we got more comfortable with each other, she started giving me information that wasn't helpful to me. Like, the manager who sat a row over — her husband was having an affair with a black woman. And the woman who was the team lead, her fiancé hits her... and so on and so on.

Oh my God, I was cornered by a gossip!

It killed the "new job honeymoon period" for me. I wasn't as excited to come to work anymore.

I tried to be polite at first.

Then I made proclamations that I had a few tough items in my queue and my work required me to focus. I avoided her conversation at all cost.

When a woman down the row moved to another division I asked my supervisor if I could move into that woman's old cubicle. My supervisor agreed knowing what I was dealing with.

Pretty soon I heard through the grapevine (it never goes away, does it?) that the gossip was telling people not to confide in me because I was a backstabber. Geesh.

That's how The Gossip operates and it was the price I paid for listening to her gossip in the first place.

Know that if you give The Gossip your ear they will take it as permission to gossip about you too. If you refuse to listen to gossip you are less likely to be gossiped about... or at the very least you'll be less likely to hear about it. ;)

The Queen

We can often think back to high school or college and easily remember girls in our past who acted this way. Many of them eventually mature, realizing that their strategy to get what they want doesn't get them what they *really* want: friendship, genuine praise, and respect.

However, some women have not yet moved past this strategy. The strategy shifts somewhat so they are not so obvious but there are telling signs that will call her out.

The Queen has to call the shots, even if she is not in a position of authority. She will make others sorry if she doesn't get her way. She may avoid official leadership positions because she doesn't want the work or responsibility, but she doesn't shy away from inserting herself in the decision-making process.

She is not a team player and collaboration is not her aim. She will fake collaboration by allowing others to make decisions she does not care about.

If she finds herself in a situation where she is not admired and adored, she will at first be baffled and then declare it "lame" or will have some other disparaging remarks about the people, the activity, the location, etc.

Some of my clients talk about a Queen in their life. A friend or family member who is only happy if everyone does what they want to do and has one set of rules for themselves and another set of rules for others.

When The Queen is happy, life is peaceful, but when she is not, it can feel like a violent electric storm came through, leaving you shaking and wondering, "What just happened?"

Do not give The Queen power over your happiness and do not become one of her subjects. Avoid her at all costs and, if it's a family member or co-worker, minimize your time with her.

Address bad behavior by sticking to the facts: what they did or said (eye rolling, sighing, interrupting, "quote their statement") and leave out assuming their attitude and intentions ("You hate this. You were trying to..."). There's almost no better way to escalate a fight than to tell someone else what they were thinking and feeling and what they were trying to do. You do not know what they were experiencing, even if you think you do. Remember those colored contact lenses?

High-energy Relationships

Now that we've gone over who to avoid or weed out of your life let's think about those you want to keep and those you want to bring into your life.

Think of the people in your life whom:

1. You get excited and happy at the thought of spending time together

2. Leave you feeling better than when you arrived

3. Make you feel appreciated and respected

4. Want your highest good

5. Are always eager to hear what you have going on

6. Congratulate you on your accomplishments, however small

7. Remain curious about you until you insist they give an update as well

These are the people you want to keep and find more of!

What would life be like if you were surrounded by people like this all the time? They were your partners, team members, friends, etc.

You do this by managing your alter ego — birds of a feather flock together! When we allow our alter ego to run the show, we are unconsciously attracting others who are also letting their alter ego run the show.

For example, if we are constantly being The Amazon Warrior, we will naturally bring out The Amazon

Warrior in others. You've experienced this: you are going about your day and then someone yells at you or accuses you of doing something and your defenses come up and, before you know it, you're in a foul mood if not in an all-out argument.

Your alter ego will also attract those who compliment your stress reaction. The Superhero will attract those who are needy or constantly have drama in their lives. Think of those who are cocooning and trying to get their energy back. They will allow a compassionate, non-judgmental Superhero to donate their energy to them. This is great and wonderful if you, as the Superhero, know where your boundaries are and protect them to prevent you from needing to cocoon too often.

Keep your alter ego in check so THE REAL YOU is the one in charge. THE REAL YOU will attract the right people to you and will be better able to identify when someone else's alter ego is running their show.

Find team members that balance you

My last thought on choosing the people who surround you is to make sure you have a mix of people who balance you. Their strengths are your weaknesses and vice versa.

If you are a people-person, make sure your team consists of people who LOVE numbers, details and minutia - and have respect for them.

Just this week I was chatting with a banker who is on the board of a non-profit organization. She was talking about the dreams the Directors of the non-profit have and it sounded exciting. However, this banker grimaced and went on to state, "They are not going to be very happy with me." When I inquired for the reason she stated, "if we're going to go to that next level, there's going to have to be changes to the infrastructure of the organization, and they won't love that part."

My response was, "That's exactly why they have you on their board. They need someone who is willing to dive into the details and tell the truth."

People who are not wired the way we are wired can be a source of conflict in our lives because it's harder to understand each other. However, if you can appreciate that they do not value the same things as you (being around people most of the time, perhaps?) you can figure out how to work together in a way that is mutually beneficial.

Type this link into your browser to access the bonus materials: **womentakingthelead.com/resources**

Final Thoughts on Part II: Qualities of those ready to GO BIG

Happy, positive

Women ready to go big are enjoyable to be around because they are aware there is so much more to be grateful for than to get upset about. This helps them manage their emotions when faced with unexpected challenges.

These women are too committed to something big to sweat the small stuff. I remember being in a leadership training when the facilitator stated, "if you are constantly getting stressed out and upset over little things, it's because your problems are not big enough. If you want less stress find a bigger problem. People who are trying to feed starving children don't get their panties in a bunch if someone cuts them off in traffic. They are too busy to stop and deal with something so inconsequential."

It was one of the biggest insights I ever got into setting priorities and finding happiness.

Cautiously optimistic

Women ready to go big are cautiously optimistic in that they know they have attended to what is in their control. They have planned, prepared and done their best.

However, they have not fooled themselves into believing that they are in control of everything. There is a lot out of their control yet these women are ready to go big, so they don't stress out over it.

Why get stressed over something they have no control over? Instead they plan for the best and go with the flow when things don't go their way. Heck, when things don't go their way they look for opportunities in the rubble and can often make something even better than what they planned.

They model for those around them the way to respond to stressful situations and because of this those around them are able to remain calm and focused.

Responsible: the ability to respond

Women ready to go big know how to assess a situation to see what is needed and will respond appropriately. They do not "stick their head in the sand" or pretend they don't know.

This does not mean they take on the work of 10 people. Responding to a need will often look like finding the right person for the job or having a quick conversation.

They are not passengers in their life; they are the drivers. If they don't like the direction they are going, they will course-correct.

A sub-set of being responsible is being socially and emotionally intelligent. First and foremost they are aware of and understand their own emotions and how to express them appropriately. They are tuned into the "vibe" in the room and the individuals.

Responsible women are constantly "reading" themselves, other people, and situations to know what is needed so they can choose how to respond.

Integrous – their word is their bond

This is a must. If you want to go big, you have to live by your word and communicate clearly and directly if forces out of your control try to keep you from it.

In order to go big, you need people to see, believe in, and help you manifest your vision. If you break your word, you will damage those relationships. If people cannot trust and rely on you to do what you say you will, they will go away.

Never, never, never, never, never use "busy" as a reason to not keep your word. Everyone is "busy" and that excuse falls flat. At best you look like you cannot manage yourself and, at worst, it looks like you pulled on the lamest excuse in the world.

If something comes up, rather than breaking your word, seek to renegotiate the agreement.

I once promised I would volunteer at an event. My sister had an emergency and needed my help. I first asked if there was anyone else she could ask and was told I was the last call. So, I renegotiated to volunteer before and after the event, rather than at the event itself.

Always be a woman of integrity.

Organized

We all go through life the way we choose to go through life, but if you want to go big you are going to have to get organized. There are too many moving parts where you are going and what will save you is organization.

Organization will increase your bandwidth and reduce stress. You don't have to wonder where everything is, when it is all going to happen, and who is responsible for what. Take a breath, it's all taken care of because you've already organized it.

I love my calendars, to-do and check lists, and procedures. The technical terms for these things are systems and processes. If this is not your strength, hire someone who has this strength and let them do what they do best: organize.

When we are organized, we create a pleasant experience for those around us. One thing we humans hate more than anything is the unknown. Organization allows you to have answers at your fingertips and that puts people at ease.

It also makes you trustworthy. You are more likely to get great opportunities when people know you have your act together.

Well spoken: clear and concise

Going big requires you to inspire others to join you on your quest. To do that, you need to describe the future you envision in a way that they can insert themselves into.

Sharing your vision of the future is just one of many things you will need to convey to make progress toward your goal. Those potential clients you know you can help? You have to be able to help them see the logic of such a decision *and* help them to emotionally weigh the opportunity you are providing with the consequences of going it alone or choosing someone else.

Careers and businesses are built on relationships and relationships are built on communication.

The more clear you are in your own mind about who you are and what your mission is, the easier it will be to put it into words for others.

Words are like magic wands — but you have to know how to wield them.

Forward thinking – solution focused, future focused

Women who are ready to go big focus on progress, improvement, solutions, and innovation if possible. They know to keep looking ahead to see what is coming and to spot opportunities that may present themselves.

They also analyze the past but only so much as to gather information on what to do next.

One exercise I like to do with my clients is a form of "looking back." We ask and answer questions that reveal what is working and what is not working. That information helps us create a strategy for moving forward that involves more of what's working and less of what's not.

Sounds simple, right? Can you imagine how many people don't look back for fear of not liking what they will see or because they think it will be a waste of time?

This is not always an easy process — there can be some squirming involved — but the information gained and the end strategy chosen always makes it worth the discomfort. There is also a lot of self-forgiveness along the way, paving the way for a better self-care strategy.

Compassionate

Lastly, women who are ready to go big have an enormous amount of compassion for themselves and others. They make a practice of facing their shame. If this makes you a little queasy, I recommend becoming a fan of Brené Brown.

By having compassion for themselves, they then create more space to have compassion for others. Remember, in the beginning of this book I referred to human beings as movie projectors projecting their inner world onto the canvas of who and what is around them? This is what I'm referring to when I say that having compassion for yourself creates more compassion in your surroundings.

When you have space for yourself, you project that out onto others and the result is that you have more space for them. This does not mean you avoid addressing issues or dealing with "bad" behavior; it means that since you're aware of what is going on around you, you

97

don't get easily upset when something outside of your control happens. Instead, you are able to address what needs to be addressed calmly, rationally, and as it happens... and that is appreciated by *everyone* involved.

What qualities do you need to develop so you are ready to go BIG? Use this worksheet to document it and create a plan to further develop this quality:

Type this link into your browser to access the bonus materials: **womentakingthelead.com/resources**

Part III:
KNOW THE GOAL AND THE PLAN

"Nothing can stop the man with the right mental attitude from achieving his goal; nothing on earth can help the man with the wrong mental attitude."

~Thomas Jefferson

Chapter 8:

Framing Your Mindset to Set Goals that Are Worthy of You

"Don't ask what the world needs. Ask what makes you come alive, and go do it. Because what the world needs is people who have come alive."

~Howard Thurman

You would never dream of building a house without a blueprint, a plan for what it would look like once it was built. You would never hire a contractor who didn't know the materials, manpower, and time it was going to take to build that house.

Is your business less important than the house you would live in? Why, oh why, would you be a leader in business and not have a clear picture of what you are building and what it's going to take to build it?

Goals, like proper nutrition, are often seen as additional work, but I've got five reasons why goals are actually the fuel to your success.

1. Goals Help You to Focus Your Attention

We are all busy. The question is what are you busy doing?

When you have clearly stated goals, preferably written and posted somewhere where you can see them, your attention is brought back to what you are trying to accomplish.

Shiny Object Syndrome is common. I can't tell you how many people I meet who believe they have a touch of Adult ADD. They don't have Adult ADD; they're not clear on what they should be focusing on in any given moment because everything seems important. As a result, everything gets a little bit of their attention and progress on any particular project or initiative is slow.

If you don't state what's important, EVERYTHING will seem important.

2. Goals Give You A Clear Sense Of When To Say "Yes" And "No"

If you are someone who has a hard time saying "no", having goals is definitely in your best interest.

If you are approached to give your time or resources, measure the request against your stated goals. You want to ask yourself, "Does this move me closer or further away from my goals?"

If it does not move you closer to your goal, the answer is, "no, for now." It's not to say you will never help the person who is approaching you; it just means that at this time, you cannot commit your time and resources to their initiative right now.

3. Goals Allow You To Measure Your Progress

This is probably one of the most important reasons for having goals. Having goals and setting milestones and time frames gives you an opportunity to gauge how you are doing against a goal.

Rather than having a vague notion of how business is doing ("I'm really busy!") you have a realistic picture from which you can make decisions.

From here you can assess what's working, what's not working, where you may need some help, or perhaps realize that you need to tweak the goal.

Having these measurements can also give you a sense of accomplishment. Because you have documented where you started from, you can also see how far you've come. This can keep the motivation up when working toward the goal becomes hard.

4. Goals Can Be Communicated To Team Members, Partners, Contractors, and Vendors

People want to help, they want to contribute.

More often than not they do not live up to this desire because they are not clear on where they can make an impact. Help them help you by sharing your goals and why you want to achieve them.

If the goal is vague (increase business, improve net profits) there's not much there for people to get inspired by nor is there a clear idea of how they can help.

Clearly crafted goals and objectives, and the reasoning behind them, motivate other people to see how they can make a difference for you in achieving your goals.

5. Bonus: Having Documented Goals Triggers the Unconscious Mind On Your Behalf

Your unconscious mind is always working. Having defined goals allows the unconscious mind to work on them, even when you are not. Your mind will constantly be looking for solutions and creative ideas to move you closer to your goal.

The more clearly stated the goal or the "problem", the better able the unconscious mind will be at finding solutions.

These solutions usually come while doing a mundane activity like washing the dishes, brushing your teeth, or going for a walk. Be ready when inspiration hits.

Goals, though they may seem tedious and stress inducing, are beneficial to you, your business, and the people around you.

Before we rush into setting goals, let's get into the right frame of mind...

Your goals, and how achievable they are, stem from the mindset that created them.

Before you create goals, or go back to tweak them, try a goal setting process that inspires and motivates you.

I typically work with entrepreneurial women around their mindset for success. I help them to identify the thoughts that are getting in the way of them growing their life and business or loving what they are invested in. My background is in psychology, and I'm one of those people who, after spending 6 years working on my undergraduate and graduate degree, realized I didn't like where my studies were taking me and so opted for something else.

I was really discouraged and disappointed with where my life had gone and when I took an entry-level corporate position, I decided I was not going to stay there for long. Except, I thrived in that position and in the next 6 years, I was promoted 5 times. It had everything to do with my mindset and my practice of setting goals.

I use a one-two punch of mindset and action goals to help my clients achieve the results they've been craving without having to white-knuckle their way through it. The tools and exercises I use help my clients identify their mindset and zero in on the actions that are going to lead them to their ultimate goal.

If you've been doing the worksheets and the exercises throughout this book, you are likely in a good place to start thinking about goals that are in alignment with who you really are — goals that are worthy of you as opposed to what your alter ego wants you to do.

It is important to set BIG goals that are worthy of you. These goals must reflect your values and focus on creating, rather than changing, a situation or relationship in your life.

For instance, a BIG goal that is worthy of you would not be to lose 10 pounds. A BIG goal that is worthy of you is to wake up in the morning feeling refreshed and energized.

Part of attaining that goal may include changing your nutrition or getting more activity in your day. However, it will call on more than diet and exercise and will have a greater ripple effect than the scale moving or your clothing feeling less snug. You may even lose the 10 pounds along the way, but your goal is to feel more refreshed and energized in the morning.

A goal that is worthy of you calls you to express the best parts of you and motivates you to keep going, even when staying on track is tough.

Make sure the goals you choose reflect your highest values and get you excited. To that end, I have another exercise for you.

Type this link into your browser to access the bonus materials: **womentakingthelead.com/resources**

Chapter 9:

SMART Goals and the Plan

"If you don't design your own life plan, chances are you'll fall into someone else's plan. And guess what they have planned for you? Not much."

~Jim Rohn

SMART goals are a certain type of goal. They are by no means the only way to set goals but what I like about SMART goals is they help you to design a framework by which you can achieve any goal.

SMART is an acronym for Specific, Measurable, Attainable, Realistic/Relevant, and Time-bound.

Specific: Who, what, and where

Measurable: How will someone know you have achieved your goal?

Attainable: You have or will have the resources you need to achieve the goal (time, money, skill level)

Realistic/Relevant: This goal is in alignment with you, your values and your greater mission/purpose

Time-bound: Completed by a specific date

You can take any goal you have and use the SMART goal process to help you get there. For instance, if I had a goal to keep my calm in upsetting situations, I would start by asking myself some questions to clarify the goal and identify some strategies.

Question: What is an "upsetting" situation?

Answer: Any situation where someone is not living up to expectations, where I feel I am being criticized, where the other person is visibly upset (raised voice, using sarcasm, snapping, etc.), or where things are not going my way.

Question: How would I know that I've achieved my goal of staying calm in upsetting situations?

Answer: I would be aware because where I would usually become angry and/or lose my temper (stop listening, interrupt, snap at people, remove myself before the conversation was over, etc.) I would instead notice my breathing, look at the situation from different angles, and start thinking of solutions, etc. If in a conversation, I would keep listening to the other person, ask questions to seek understanding, and stay in the conversation until a solution was found or a plan was in place. I would also know I've achieved my goal if I did not need to "recover" after the situation was over.

Question: What would help me achieve a level of control over my emotions that allows me to stay calm?

Answer: Getting more sleep, having fewer "obligations" in my life — a more relaxed calendar, meditation, and more walks in nature to name a few. (These are strategies).

Question: Of those strategies, which would I like to take on first?

Answer: I think they all tie together. If I got to bed earlier, I'd have time to meditate in the morning. If I practiced meditation and became more skilled at calming my mind, I would find it easier to calm my mind at night, and especially those times when I wake up in the middle of the night and my mind starts to race. If I remove some of the "obligations" that I no longer have a desire for off my calendar, I would have more time to go for nature walks.

I now have four strategies for my ultimate goal of staying calm in upsetting situations. Each one of these strategies can now be turned into a SMART goal.

For example:

I will be getting 7.5-8 hours of sleep each night by December 31st.

I will be meditating for at least 15 minutes a day within 60 days.

I will resign my volunteer position at XYZ Association by the end of the year.

I will go for a walk on the trail at least 4 times a week.

Some other examples of SMART goals are: make $5,000 more this year than last year, lose 20 pounds in 20 weeks, or take an out of state vacation that doesn't involve visiting family in the next 6 months.

To increase the likelihood that you'll achieve your SMART goals and eventually your ultimate goal we're going to document those goals and create an action plan with milestones that you will hit along the way. You'll also plug in celebrations and rewards for hitting the milestones and get an accountability partner. Having another person who will witness your challenges and successes will motivate you to stay on track.

The satisfaction you feel from achieving your goals is directly related to how well you choose the right goals for you, ones that stretch you a bit, and how well you execute your plan. Give yourself the gift of choosing goals worthy of you, the ones that, upon reaching, will have you fist pumping and that feeling of joy washing over you.

Type this link into your browser to access the bonus materials: **womentakingthelead.com/resources**

Chapter 10:

Staying Motivated as You Work to Achieve Those Goals

"Why are you going to choose failure when success is an option?"

~Jillian Michaels

If ever you find yourself struggling, I've got ten of my favorite tips that can help make it easier to achieve those goals you've defined.

You CAN do it. Remember how you learned to walk? Step by step. Tackle your goals step by step - and you'll be well on your way to success!

10 Things You Must Do to Meet Your Goals

1. Create a Personal Mission Statement.

Define what you're about. What do you value? What are your goals? What is your purpose? Be specific. Be honest with yourself. When you're not, you lose your integrity. And as we lose our integrity, we lose our power.

2. Surround yourself with positive doers.

Being around negativity pulls you down and sucks the energy right out of you. Being around positive, uplifting people puts a shine on your disposition. You feel better and are more motivated! Better yet, surround yourself with positive doers who have goals similar to your goals. You can mutually learn from each other, the successes and the failures, have someone to be accountable to (so important!) and motivate each other to keep going when staying on track with your goals become challenging.

3. Get creative.

Everyone is different – and we all approach things differently, too. Be different in the techniques you use to meet your goals! Talk to a trusted advisor. Meditate.

Sleep on it. Ask for help. There are plenty of methods to help you achieve your goals but you need to invest some energy to find what is going to work for you.

4. Give thanks.

Learn to appreciate the good things in your life. Expressing gratitude makes you feel better, both physically and emotionally. Start a gratitude journal. Write down 3 things each day that you are thankful for. You'll find yourself becoming happier and healthier!

5. Let go of the past. Release what no longer serves you.

Stop carrying around that excess negative baggage. There is great power in forgiving. As Melissa Kirk wrote, "When we let go, we fly. Even if we just take a couple of flaps and end up two feet away from where we were, not sure if we have the courage to try again, we still made a change, one that might have wide-ranging implications, if we just had the patience to let the ripples wash up against distant shores."

6. Quit worrying what others will think.

When we rely more on what other people think rather than relying on our own values, we increase the chances of making bad decisions. Get comfortable with yourself. Living with a mindset of "what will they think of me?" is one of the fastest ways to pop out of alignment with your core values. Honestly ask yourself, does it really matter – really – what other people think?

7. Make your action plan easy to execute.

Break all of your goals down into baby steps and daily habits. In his book, *The Slight Edge*, Jeff Olson explains that the same simple actions that take us from near failure to moderate success are the same actions that, if maintained over time, would take us from moderate success to wild success. They are our daily habits that either move us toward our goal or away from our goal. What are the daily habits that will take you toward your goal?

8. Know when to cut your losses.

Don't waste your valuable time persisting in goals that are beyond reach. Hopefully by following the SMART process, you had an opportunity to consider how achievable the goal is, but sometimes we set goals based on a hope that certain things out of our control will fall into place. Or life throws you a curve ball. First, look to see of you can recover from the unexpected changes and if not, make peace with it and adjust or let go of your goal.

9. Take responsibility for your actions.

Don't blame anyone for your actions. It's a waste of time, cultivates a good deal of stress, and in the end, nothing is gained. Own up to your accomplishments – and failures. There are lessons to be learned in both!

10. Stop and smell the roses.

Celebrate your accomplishments! Recognize positive steps you've taken and reward yourself. Celebrating what you've achieved is an important part of the goal-setting process. Take the time to think about your achievement...how exciting it is...and how it is a springboard to higher success!

"Great things are not done by impulse, but by a series of small things brought together. " ~Vincent VanGogh

Yes, you really can achieve your goals! Envision them, write them down, work towards them each day, each moment, and you will see yourself transform. Each little step of accomplishment brings forth a new you...and each step you take will be higher than the next...to the day you can say, "I did it!"

Chapter 11:

Common Pitfalls of Ambitious Entrepreneurial Women

"No one can make you feel inferior without your consent."

~Eleanor Roosevelt

Have you fallen off track, but are at a loss for what happened? Here are some reasons why you may be falling behind, and what you can do to get yourself back on track.

You Are Still Trying to Do Most of the Work

If you set a big goal (and congratulations if you did) the whole point was to stretch yourself. You cannot achieve that goal by being the same leader you were last year.

A General can't wage a war in the trenches and neither can you. You need to keep your eye on the big picture. Of course there will be times you need to roll up your sleeves and pitch in, but it should not be the norm.

You are better served developing the skills of the people around you, so they get better at doing those tasks.

The word of the day is delegate. Learn to let go of the control, allow others a learning curve, and focus on the tasks that only YOU can do. The tasks you know the company needs you to focus on.

You Are Still Saying "Yes" When You Want To Say "No"

You may have cleared some things off your schedule to allow you to focus on your goals but you are finding all new commitments on your calendar. Time is no sooner freed up than someone comes along and asks if they can have a chunk of it.

You know that time is meant for something else, but you can't stop yourself, and you give it away. Now you're at square one and you don't have time to work on your goal. You may find yourself saying, "I'm just so busy!"

Here I'm going to tell you to take responsibility. It's your calendar and YOU are in control of it. You need to take an honest look at it and decide if what you see on your calendar is more important than your goal.

Is your calendar an honest reflection of what is important in your life?

Chances are there are some meetings you are taking just to be "nice." Could a one-hour coffee meet-up be changed to a half-hour phone call, also saving you travel-time? Is it something that can come off your calendar altogether?

Did you agree to take on a volunteer position but it really doesn't work right now for you to do so?

Start the cleanup process again and start carving out blocks of time on your calendar that you consider etched in stone. Nothing that is less important than your goal is allowed to trump that time. Give that time-block a title that reflects its importance to remind you of this intention if the urge to say "yes" pops up.

You've Experienced Some Setbacks and You Are Not as Enthusiastic as You Were at the Beginning

Nobody loves to fail but failure is a part of the learning process. The question is what did you learn from these setbacks? How can they help you?

Setbacks are often opportunities, but only if we are willing to see and relate to them as opportunities.

If something isn't working, isn't it better to know at the outset than to learn later in the process, when changes will not be as easily implemented? What a gift!

If you can change your perspective on challenges, failures, and setbacks, you will change your response to them and that will save you a lot of time and energy. You will remain enthusiastic, or become more so, because you won't relate to the event as a reason to give up.

Remember, Thomas Edison had about 1,000 failed attempts at inventing the light bulb before he succeeded. He never related to his failed attempts as a reason to quit. They were experiments that informed his next attempt. As a result, he discovered several dozen other inventions and key scientific principles.

If any of the three reasons for not hitting milestones sound familiar, you know what you need to do: delegate, set boundaries around your time, and change your interpretation of failure.

If you need help with any of this don't hesitate to contact me so you're not feeling left behind as the year continues.

The Accomplished Community

You and I have come to the end of this book and you may be left feeling like it was not enough.

In my experience, if I get a lot out of a book or a program I want to be able to chat with others who are reading the same book or doing the same program. I know I get more out of the experience and put what I've learned into action if I'm having ongoing conversations about the material.

I would also want to learn more and be in the author's world to get a peek into how they were designing their days. I wanted to be a part of a community of like-minded people because I knew I would go further faster with their influence and guidance.

As much as we may tend to "go it alone" it's not something we really want to do – it's more of a default way of doing things that we slip into unless we're given an offer to do otherwise.

Well I'm offering you another option.

I've created **The Accomplished Community** for you to continue the work you've begun and to meet and chat with other women like you who are working through the same material, having similar insights and challenges, and who also have big goals they are determined to accomplish.

Type this link into your browser to get more information:

womentakingthelead.com/accomplished-community

Made in the USA
Columbia, SC
18 April 2018